D1475816

DARLING VULGARITY

Books by Michael Waters

Darling Vulgarity 2006
Parthenopi: New and Selected Poems 2001
Green Ash, Red Maple, Black Gum 1997
Bountiful 1992
The Burden Lifters 1989
Anniversary of the Air 1985
Not Just Any Death 1979
Fish Light 1975

Editor:

Contemporary American Poetry (with A. Poulin, Jr.) Eighth Edition, 2006;
   Seventh Edition, 2001
Perfect in Their Art: Poems on Boxing from Homer to Ali (with Robert Hedin) 2003
A. Poulin, Jr. Selected Poems 2001
Dissolve to Island: On the Poetry of John Logan 1984

DARLING VULGARITY

POEMS BY

MICHAEL WATERS

AMERICAN POETS CONTINUUM SERIES, NO. 101

BOA Editions, Ltd. ❋ Rochester, NY ❋ 2006

First Edition
06 07 08 09   7 6 5 4 3 2 1

Publications by BOA Editions, Ltd.—a not-for-profit corporation under section 501 (c) (3) of
the United States Internal Revenue Code—are made possible with the assistance of grants from
the Literature Program of the New York State Council on the Arts;
the Literature Program of the National Endowment for the Arts; County of Monroe, NY;
the Lannan Foundation for support of the Lannan Translation Selection Series;
Sonia Raiziss Giop Charitable Foundation; Mary S. Mulligan Charitable Trust;
Rochester Area Community Foundation; Arts & Cultural Council for Greater Rochester;
Steeple-Jack Fund; Elizabeth F. Cheney Foundation; Eastman Kodak Company;
Chesonis Family Foundation; Ames-Amzalak Memorial Trust in memory of Henry Ames,
Semon Amzalak and Dan Amzalak; and contributions from many individuals nationwide.

See Colophon on page 96 for special individual acknowledgments.

Cover Design: Daphne Poulin-Stofer
Cover Art: "Sitting Angel" by Alexey Terenin, oil on board, 2004, courtesy of the author
Interior Design and Composition: Richard Foerster
Manufacturing: McNaughton & Gunn, Lithographers
BOA Logo: Mirko

Library of Congress Cataloging-in-Publication Data

Waters, Michael, 1949–
  Darling vulgarity / Michael Waters.– 1st ed.
      p. cm. – (American poets continuum series ; no. 101)
  ISBN 1–929918–85–2 (pbk. : alk. paper)
  I. Title. II. Series: American poets continuum series ; v. 101.

  PS3573.A818D37 2006
  813'.54–dc22

2006007145

BOA Editions, Ltd.
Thom Ward, Editor
David Oliveiri, Chair
A. Poulin, Jr., President & Founder (1938–1996)
260 East Avenue, Rochester, NY 14604
www.boaeditions.org

NATIONAL
ENDOWMENT
FOR THE ARTS

State of the Arts
NYSCA

CONTENTS

13 *A Note on the Poems*

❋ **I**

17 Black Olives
19 Fauns Fleeing Before an Automobile
20 Poinciana
21 Wedding Dress
22 Erotic Roman Antiquities
23 Miserere
24 Bosporus
26 American Eel

❋ **II**

31 Eddie's Parrot
32 Family Outing
33 What•ev•er
35 The Bicycle and the Soul

❋ **III**

45 The Tether
47 Deep-Sea Sponge
48 Scarabs
49 Processional
51 Commerce
53 2 Revelation 1:2
54 Who Are These Ravens
56 Ossuary
57 The Crusades
58 Backrub

IV

63 Making Love at the Frost Place
64 Isamu Noguchi
65 Junkie Tempo
66 Sonnet for Strummer
67 Balthus
68 Pavese
69 *La Bohème*: The New England Marionettes
71 Raymond Carver
73 Elegant Lady
75 Blue Ankle

 V

79 Green Sweater
81 Tzaddikim Nistarim
83 The Book of Constellations

✳

86 Notes
88 Acknowledgments
91 About the Author
96 Colophon

✳

for Kiernan
DV

. . . niceness rules out the mysterious, blunt, fierce, and unexpected side of people and things.
—Balthus

Darling Vulgarity

A NOTE ON THE POEMS

First they understood nothing, then had to unlearn even that—

> *like the Diving School students*
> *strapped into scuba gear—tanks belts masks hoses fins—*
> *flailing like caterpillars at the bottom of the pool*
> *while the Divemaster prowled the perimeter*
> *cupping hands & shouting into the shallows:*
> *"Breathe! Will you fuckers learn to breathe!"*

I

BLACK OLIVES

In those days while my then-wife
taught English to a mustached young nurse who hoped to join
her uncle's practice in Queens,
I'd sip gin on our balcony and listen to her
read aloud from the phrasebook,
then hear the student mimic, slowly, *Where does it hurt?*
then my wife repeat those words
so the woman might enunciate each syllable,
until I could no longer
bear it, so I'd prowl the Ambelokipi district
attempting to decipher
titles emblazoned on marquees—*My Life As A Dog*,
Runaway Train, *Raging Bull*—
then stroll past dark shops that still sold only one item—
kerosene, soap, cheese, notebooks—
to step down into the shop that sold olives, only
olives in barrels riddling
a labyrinth of dank aisles and buttressing brick walls.
I'd sidle among squat drums,
fingering the fruit, thumbing their inky shine, their rucked
skins like blistered fingertips,
their plump flesh, the rough salts needling them, judging their cowled
heft, biding my time. Always
I'd select a half-kilo of the most misshapen,
wrinkled and blackest olives
sprung from the sacred rubble below Mt. Athos, then
had to shout "Fuck Kissinger!"
three times before the proprietor would allow me
to make my purchase, then step
back out into the smut-stirred Athens night to begin
the slow stroll home, bearing now

my little sack of woe, oil seeping through brown paper,
each olive brought toward my mouth
mirroring lights flung from marquees and speeding taxis,
each olive burning its coal-
flame of bitterness and history into my tongue.

FAUNS FLEEING BEFORE AN AUTOMOBILE

What young couple, leaving the affair, hasn't seen them,
the fauns, leaping vast foliaged silences,
slashed momentarily by headlights:
their yellow, goatlike, sin-slit eyes,
their scabrous haunches,
the dull gloss of cloven hoof as it disappears in brush?

We had been arguing, slightly drunk,
about ex-lovers with flirtatious
gestures, about low murmurs in corners—
suddenly they appeared, three or four,
a muscular rush among brambles, a furious blur, almost-
human creatures swept underworld by light.

Our rampant voices stilled then—
that awestruck *hush*,
creation's tentative pause—
then only the tick of wipers urging our arrival
home, the undressing, the desperate
confusions of flesh—mine or yours?—

while fauns huddled in leaf shadow,
rubbing together their burr-riddled, filth-smeared
flanks, nuzzling coarse necks, still
spooked by the splendor
kindling God's wild eye, still
catching their terrible breath.

POINCIANA

The man who offered one hundred dollars
to watch me undress my wife wasn't pocked
or breathy like some B-movie voyeur,
but had approached us in the hotel bar
and improvised almost perfect English.
His burnished leather loafers and blazer
sparked elegance amid rumpled shirttails
and parrot-hued, flimsy sheaths and sandals.
Tipsy from fingers of flaming liqueurs
that beckon only in foreign countries,
sun-flushed and giddy with tropical spunk,
we let him swim the runnel of perfume
coursing the lobby, leading to our room.
On our balcony, I unzipped her dress,
slipped it off shoulders to expose her breasts—
then pool at her feet in a tinsel shimmer
as though she were stepping like Susannah
from her garden bath of spices and oils.
Whose fantasy this was, I can't recall.
The man knelt on tiles, weeping from one eye.
My nude wife trembled in jazz-laden breeze.
I tapped one finger along the ivory
keys of her spine, not knowing what came next,
or how to strike our shame
before money exchanged hands
or when waking next morning wild with thirst.

WEDDING DRESS

That Halloween I wore your wedding dress,
our children spooked & wouldn't speak for days.
I'd razored taut calves smooth, teased each blown tress,
then—lipsticked, mascaraed, & self-amazed—
shimmied like a starlet on the dance floor.
I'd never felt so sensual before—
Catholic schoolgirl & neighborhood whore.
In bed, dolled up, undone, we fantasized:
we clutched & fused, torn twins who'd been denied.
You were my shy groom. Love, I was your bride.

EROTIC ROMAN ANTIQUITIES

Naples

Even in the museum we held hands—

    like those schoolchildren
    sporting yellow tees & blue bandannas,
    each clasping a partner, noisy little clones
    steered away from the exhibit by their tutor—

before glass cases lit like store windows
displaying their goods: penises
with bells hanging from them, penises
with legs, penises with wings and, in one instance,
a penis with bells, legs, *and* wings.

I'd forgotten that exhibition of erotic Roman antiquities
until this morning, when I asked, "Why do you sleep so much?"
and, smiling, you replied:
                "In my sleep, I forgive you."

MISERERE

We're bathing together when Alina kneels in steam
to reveal crimped flaps of skin,
drawn shades the surgeons have fashioned: system of pulleys
worked by little metal wheels
screwed into each shoulder. She rolls them with a finger:
the shades scroll: I gaze through her,
through windows opened in her chest, past icy tendrils
scrawling abandoned gardens
where seven unborn sisters, hands joined in a circle,
attempt to sing a sacred
cycle by Górecki or Pärt, a healing chorale
that resurrects starved finches,
lifts fallen fruit back to black branches, replenishes
green in winter-scorched grasses.
Their voices swell through each scar-rimmed oval. O, she says,
look: they've taken both my breasts.
Yes, I reply, but listen: hasn't God replaced them
with such glorious music.

BOSPORUS

Zigzagging eighteen miles north
from the Sea of Marmara to the Black Sea, we lean
toward Europe on our left, toward
Asia failing now, at dusk, on our right, two souls tugged
toward each point of the compass . . .
toward the past with its previous lives, toward the future
with its final, unswerving
destination: death. Or not: hadn't we visited
the House of the Virgin where
Mary had thrummed patience after the resurrection,
Christ's tomb exhaling only
foreign fragrance, her son's cerements twisting in dust?
Swathed in blue, she coaxed savory
& dill in her garden, wheedled fierce daylilies while
awaiting airy summons.
Outside the house, tourists thronged the cobblestones, knotted
invocations to fence wire:
Our Lady grant world peace; heal me; whisper the winning
numbers into my deaf ear.
They scribbled pleas on scarves, soiled bandages, underwear,
streamers of toilet tissue,
their thwarted desires blue-blacked in the common language
of desperation, in linked
sequences of DNA that conspire to keep us
ordinary. *Hail, Mary. . . .*
Here on the Bosporus, where two continents begin
their inexorable drift,
their seismic fragmentation toward solitude & ruin,
I consecrate my offering:
that scrap torn from a battered Lonely Planet guidebook,

inscribed, then crumpled & tucked
into some postulant's limp panty hose, its one word
faded now by sunlight, its
single looped prayer commencing its formal dispersal:
my howl, my thirst, my tether:
your name grown pale on paper, becoming breeze that salts
our lips, becoming weather.

AMERICAN EEL

Anguilla rostrata

My quick & kindling daughter
bolted ahead as we approached the abandoned wharf,
light flashing off burial
mounds slick with silt & salt marshes raveling the bay.
We were not quite family.
My lover had flown down from New England, elegant
in haute couture even here
among bridle paths & planks warping over runnels,
spiked heels daubed with mud, bangles
chiming like birdcall, each gesture sparked & erratic,
the air barbed with a coursing
electricity, a nervous energy that drew
admirers into its light,
then burned them, as she exhausted herself & her friends
with helpless consummations.
"We're not that kind of people," she'd admonish her son,
who propped one elbow upon
the table or let a shirttail droop, then lick her thumb
to rub away a freckle.
Suddenly my daughter let loose a shrill *ewwww!*—we heard,
below that sour pitch, a dim
sorption like soapsuds sieving through a wooden bucket:
eels stranded in low tide, mud
eels thrashing the river's bottom, urging their flaccid
intimations forward inch
by blunt inch before doubling back on themselves, tugging
their viscous sleeves through throbbing
clumps of sisters tangled like fishing line. Creation's
rank exhalations—the eels'
frenzied upheavals & shudderings—freighted the air.

"Let's get the fuck outta here!"
yelped my daughter. My fiancée glared, then turned away
to let me wrestle the flaw.
Speckled paths & murmurous streams recalled the famous
forest scene: Dimmesdale reveling
in arousal when he quit the moral wilderness
where Hester Prynne had undone
her hair to allow its sexual waters to bathe him,
the reverend ready to teach
Puritan children how to curse, or torch the virgin's
innocence with some verbal
"germ of evil," one coarse utterance to make her flinch.
"Bad word," I wagged my finger
as my daughter looked chastened, as my lover eased back
into our perfect future,
"but"—I couldn't help myself—"you used it correctly."
I hugged my girl, my darling
vulgarity. We *are* that kind of people. Eels seethed,
convulsive balls of gristle,
then boiled through mud flats to rupture the river's veneer.

II

EDDIE'S PARROT

As he jiggled the key in the lock
each evening he returned home from work,
his cued, quick parrot began to squawk,
Where's Eddie? Where's Eddie? Where's Eddie?
till my uncle barreled through the door—
Honey, I'm home! (his vaudevillian's joke)—
to let that straight man chew one knuckle.
Then Eddie died, and Aunt Anna swore
that chatterbox screeched rote rhetoric
every time she trudged back from the store,
creating a tenth circle of hell,
Where's Eddie? never allowing her
a moment's respite from grief, though she
told that feathery philosopher
He's dead, Eddie's dead. But such a swell-
educated Hegel couldn't quit—
Where's Eddie? Where's Eddie? Where's Eddie?—
and Anna, grown foulmouthed, psychotic,
He's dead, he's goddamn dead!—till one dusk
she snapped and stormed that Catskill comic's
stage, rattling bars till the stunned parrot
sprawled from his spotlit plank, his scrambled
brain dumb now among split seeds, carrot
shreds, such sad confetti!—the silence
sweet, my prankster uncle gone for good.

FAMILY OUTING

1938

Against the tiled wall of the Hoyt-Schermerhorn station
a man was hurting a girl—
how my father always recalled it—so, off duty,
my grandfather nabbed the thug,
hauled him upstairs, then whistled to alert the precinct.
Soon a buddy cop huffed up
to cuff the creep who leaned in close to whisper some filth
into my grandmother's ear.
She swayed on stilts, drained white. "*What* did he say to you, May?"—
not so much a question, while
with eyes shut she implored the saints to undo her shame.
"Walk the wee ones home," he spat,
and as she pleaded, "George, don't!" she ushered them away.
But my father snuck one glance:
wrists still cuffed behind his back, the punk perched at the top
of the steep, iron-rimmed steps
descending into the churning bowels of Brooklyn Heights,
my grandfather's shadow wound
tight behind—palms poised—his flatfoot pal nowhere in sight.

WHAT•EV•ER—

the three syllables my father exhaled
   to punctuate each shrug,
      his secular version of *Jesus Christ!*

once surgeons had scraped away
   the last black cells of belligerence;
      later channeled from some afterlife

through the sewn-with-invisible-thread
   lips of my mother when her compulsive,
      trivial dicta had been defied,

who never tired of quoting St. Teresa
   to any creature who'd listen:
      "We cannot deal violently with God."

One morning my father phoned
   to tell me he'd gotten smashed
      at their annual Christmas bash,

so my mother had begun
   yanking bottles off the well-stocked
      bar to empty them into the sink—

my father stunned, then spiteful:
   "Fine. I'll help you!"—both of them at 2 A.M.
      splashing booze down the drain,

1.75 liter bottles of Johnnie Walker Black,
   Tanqueray, Absolut, Jameson, the dozen
      liqueurs like auras flaming from fingers,

even the Italian table wines
　　in green glass scalloped like fish,
　　　　till not a single shot remained, not one sip,

the Formica counters cluttered with empties.
　　Then they marched to bed and slept.
　　　　"How'd you feel this morning, Dad?"

"I had to drive to the state store
　　and blow four hundred bucks on booze!
　　　　Jesus . . . your mother . . . whatever."

I hear the word now from the mouths
　　of students, dim dears who insist
　　　　a poem means what you want it to mean,

so I begin to articulate the formal
　　gestures of prosody—ictus and breve,
　　　　their rigorous precisions; the subtle

insistence of resonance and rhyme;
　　strict syllabic scaffoldings;
　　　　the function of nuance

and the integrity of the poetic line—
　　until they cross their eyes and shrug
　　　　(who can blame them?)

while in the back row some bored Ed. major
　　with his baseball cap screwed on backwards
　　　　groans in my father's voice: *Yeah. Whatever.*

THE BICYCLE AND THE SOUL

The Bicycle

Spring 1965: I speed my bike down the Eliot Avenue hill one Saturday afternoon on my way to confession at Resurrection Ascension Church on Woodhaven Boulevard. I'm a happy kid—several New York Mets have moved into Middle Village, including my hero, rookie Ron Swoboda, the guy who charges forward from left field at the crack of the bat, then has to turn around and run back to make the catch *at precisely the point where he'd been standing*. His dubious gift is to transform every pop fly into a line drive, to transform, however briefly, his awkward, loping gait into Willie Mays' graceful, panther-like stride. While I know Middle Village takes its name from being situated between cemeteries, I'm only vaguely aware that its development took place under the mistaken notion that Negroes would be afraid to live there. "I had a terror—since September—," wrote Emily Dickinson in a letter to Thomas Wentworth Higginson, "I could tell to none—and so I sing, as the Boy does by the Burying Ground—because I am afraid." As I coast into the church's parking lot, I realize that I've forgotten my lock, so I prop the bike against one wall and race down the basement steps to the confessional.

"Bless me father for I have sinned," I begin, and rasp through a half-dozen minor moral violations in thirty seconds, then await my penance and absolution. But there's only silence. "Father . . . ?" I whisper.

His voice has an edge to it, a tone that conveys both weariness and impatience. "You sound like you're in a hurry."

"I *am* in a hurry, Father. I left my bike upstairs with no lock, and somebody might steal it." I fidget on both knees and drum unclasped fingers on the mesh screen through which I breathe my adolescent anxiety.

There is another silence now during which I imagine Negroes or Gypsies or Jews or those *West Side Story*-type hoodlums who swell the public schools—outsiders who had been described as wolf and fox to my Pinocchio on an almost daily basis by the Sisters of St. Joseph at St. Martin of Tours Elementary School—dancing around the flames of my burning bicycle before somehow managing to pedal away, all of them balanced atop the fiery

Schwinn like some circus troupe from Hell.

I understand the sources of such urban, Bosch-like scenarios even as I reject them. Still, someone might steal my bike. From the murkiness of the confessional the priest's voice freights the air with moral gravity. "And which concerns you more—your bicycle or your soul?"

I hear myself breathe, respiration/inspiration. Had I read *Huckleberry Finn* by then, and did I admire Huck's refusal, despite the burden of his moral and social contract, to betray Jim? Yes. Was I already a boxing fan, enthralled by the integrity and arrogance of Cassius Clay's reinvention of himself as Muhammad Ali? Yes. How often does a boy have the opportunity to make a decision—right or wrong, right *and* wrong—that will deepen his vast privacy, his sense of himself in relation to the world? Having made the right decision, Huck accepted his damnation. His charge was a human being. I had only a bicycle. *Still, someone might steal my bike.*

"I'm outta here," I shrug, then take the stairs two at a time into the April slant of light, hop onto my bicycle, and struggle uphill to inform my parents that I am through with churchgoing, keeping to myself the fact that, like Huck, I have willingly consigned my soul to the eternal flames.

Allen Ginsberg

In October 1966, Allen Ginsberg read his poems at Town Hall in mid-Manhattan. I'd seen Ginsberg that summer, sitting cross-legged on the floor of the Strand Bookstore at Broadway and 12th, where Walt Whitman had posed for photographs in the studio of George C. Cox on April 15, 1887. Ginsberg had stacked several small columns of books around him, creating a private space to inhabit amid the hubbub, and I'd kept my respectful distance. I was sixteen. My date for his reading that fall evening was Linda Horr, nineteen, a go-go dancer at a club in the Village. I'd met her several weeks before at a party where I'd swigged Old Mr. Boston Lemon-Flavored Gin from a half-pint bottle, not using a glass so that everyone could see what was making me choke with each sip. We'd spoken briefly, but after she left I asked our host for her number, and when I phoned, she pretended to remember me and agreed to come hear Ginsberg. I couldn't believe my luck. She was nineteen! A go-go dancer! And that name! I am not making up a word of this.

I'd spent the summer of 1966 writing pornography for C.A.D. Publishers. I'd responded to an ad in *The Village Voice*, **Writers Wanted**, and someone phoned to arrange an interview. My parents were perplexed. I had nothing but a few high school research papers on *Pygmalion* and *The Red Pony* and *Death Be Not Proud* to demonstrate my skills, yet I took the F train into the city and sat before a somewhat bemused executive who told me I'd be paid $1,200 for a pornographic novel of approximately 120 pages: ten chapters of twelve pages each, or twelve chapters of ten pages each, it was up to me (*I* was the writer), so long as the characters rampantly engaged in sex on every page.

I can't imagine what that fellow thought when I entered his office. Sixteen, I looked thirteen, and I assured him I'd had *plenty* of experience, writing and otherwise, to qualify me for the position. He didn't doubt it, he told me, giving me a wink, and mentioned that if his secretary returned from lunch before our interview ended, he'd have her blow me right there in the office. I quickly checked my watch. I wasn't sure precisely what "blow" meant, nor was I convinced that I wanted to be there when she returned. My prospective employer gave me several of his company's books, told me to write a first chapter and send it to him, and if he liked it—why wouldn't he?— I'd become a C.A.D. author and could begin churning out the porn and counting the big bucks. I was on my way.

That guy must have howled as he told his buddies about me that afternoon and for many years after. *His secretary!*—what a great touch! Yet there I was, on the F train again, returning to Queens in mid-June, school over, ready to announce to my parents that I'd secured a summer job as a pornographer. I looked at the books he'd given me and grew embarrassed that their lurid covers—illustrations of topless young women who seemed to be exercising in front of a mirror while a well-dressed gentleman watched from a doorway—and explicit titles weren't concealed in a paper bag. I browsed through one book, several pages of oral sex, and felt my face flush as I read the climactic sentence, "Billy barked joyously," not having realized until that moment that our protagonist was a handsome collie. Still, it didn't occur to me that I might be out of my element. I went home and, good writer, got to work.

The chapter contained breasts "like scoops of vanilla ice cream topped with maraschino cherries" and flesh that tasted "like some strange, delicious cream cheese." One man exhibited an erection that "rose like bread in an Italian baker's oven." My bent, apparently, had more to do with multiculturalism and the culinary arts than with similes and sex. I submitted my spicy sentences to the publisher, but a response never came. If one had, it would have been too late—my career as a pornographer had been ended by my mother.

I came home from skateboarding one afternoon to find her furious, pacing the house, anticipating my arrival.

"I saw what you wrote!"

"You saw what I . . . ?"

"I read your book. Filth!"

"My book . . . you read my . . . oh. Oh! What do you mean . . . *where* did you read my book?"

"I found it in your room."

"*My room!* You were in my room!"

But she was having none of my adolescent indignation. "I was emptying your wastebasket and saw what you wrote. Are you crazy? That's it. That's *it!*"

"I told you I had the job. You knew what I was doing."

"I didn't know *that*. Who could know that? What would the neighbors think?"

Although she'd converted to Catholicism when she'd married my father, my mother was still Jewish, especially when she was upset.

"The neighbors?"

Here my mother supplied an example of her pretzel logic. "Suppose I'd put that filth in the trash, and a dog knocked over the garbage can, and the wind blew the papers down the street, and a neighbor picked them up? What then?"

I was trying to follow this Rube Goldberg variation.

"And your teachers. What about them?"

My teachers were Marist Brothers at Christ the King High School. It hadn't occurred to me that sex would interest them, plus they didn't live anywhere near us.

"That's it," my mother repeated. "Forget it. *You're* never going to be any writer."

Now, a few months later, Linda Horr and I sat in Town Hall. She had taken my hand in hers, leaned into my shoulder, and breathed into my ear. Allen Ginsberg was about to read. A prayer rug had been centered on the otherwise bare stage, and a microphone bent to knee level. Ginsberg appeared with no introduction, sat cross-legged, bowed his head to the applause, then began to recite his poems. I was struck by his gentle manner, by one finger, held in the air like a miniature baton, that seemed to conduct his voice, and by the way his own lines of poetry seemed to excite him. He also sang several poems by William Blake, accompanying himself on harmonium, then was joined by Peter Orlovsky, whom he had married in 1954, on finger cymbals for the Hare Krishna chant. The audience swayed like sunflowers. Then very quickly it was over. Ginsberg had kept looking at the clock during the performance—he must have rented the venue for a couple hours only. Linda Horr and I walked up the aisle toward the exit, still holding hands and chanting, "Hare Krishna Hare Krishna Krishna Krishna Hare Rama. . . ."

Outside the building on 43rd Street, Ginsberg and Orlovsky leaned against their Volkswagen van. They smiled at us as we told them how much we'd enjoyed the reading. They kept smiling at us. I introduced my date and mentioned, thinking to impress them, that she was a go-go dancer in the Village. They just kept smiling. Then Ginsberg asked, "Would you like to come back to our apartment for soup?"

Soup?

I should have realized at that moment that Ginsberg, Beat poet, pop icon, gay activist, cohort of Bob Dylan, *enfant terrible*, was, most of all, a Jewish mother. *Soup?* He could have been *my* Jewish mother. We politely declined his invitation and left, but not before Ginsberg wrote his phone number in a small notebook, tore out the page, and handed it to me. "Call me," he smiled. Linda Horr and I huddled to the subway, and I was so happy that I never phoned her again.

Linda Horr, if you read this, forgive me. I have thought at times that I must have made you up, like Poe's Ligeia. You were my first muse, and I can't recall my early, fumbling attempts at poetry without thinking of you twirling around me that cold fall evening in Times Square, below the Pepsi-Cola waterfall display, chanting "Hare Krishna" and making me feel intelligent, sophisticated, and sexy, rather than awkward and pimply. You allowed me to imagine myself beyond the boundaries of my body, and to create a privacy and begin to inhabit it, the way Walter Whitman, Brooklyn journalist, must have invented Walt Whitman the poet.

For the next few months, until I discovered that it was listed in the Manhattan directory, I thought I must be the only boy in New York City who had Allen Ginsberg's phone number tucked in his wallet. But I never called him either. I'd told my parents about the invitation, so whenever I was late coming home from a track meet or the library or a movie, my father, a fireman, would start shouting at my mother, "I bet he's gone to see that Ginsberg guy!" and my mother would start to cry.

I saw Allen Ginsberg only once after that, at an antiwar rally in Bryant Park the following month. When I arrived at the park that afternoon, I spotted him sitting on steps leading up to the makeshift stage, and slipped past some police barricades to sit next to him. He was scribbling in his notebook and he stopped to look at me, nodded hello, placed his hand over mine for a moment, then returned to his work. When he climbed onto the platform to read, I ghosted into the crowd, sixteen, anonymous, wondering if Ginsberg's benediction had somehow countered my mother's unwitting curse.

Robert Lowell

During 1970–71, while attending the University of Nottingham, I sometimes hitchhiked south to London to spend a few hours in Bernard Stone's Turret Books where American poets gathered on Saturdays—I remember meeting Marilyn Hacker there—then head to the hipper Compendium Bookshop at Camden High. Once I attempted to purchase a copy of Poet Laureate Cecil Day-Lewis's *Selected Poems* there, but the proprietor refused to sell it to me, insisting that I purchase several other books instead, including John Weiners' *Nerves*, Ted Berrigan's *In the Early Morning Rain*, and Edward Dorn's *Gunslinger 1 & 2*, all published in England in 1970.

One Saturday the lorry driver who picked me up told me that the BBC had reported the death of an important American poet. Who? He couldn't remember. We played a guessing game for the next three hours—Berryman? Sexton? Lowell?—until he dropped me off, and Bernard Stone allowed that it was Ogden Nash.

Robert Lowell had accepted a teaching appointment at the University of Essex that fall, and was scheduled to read his poems at the nearby University of Leicester. When I arrived with a few other American students on the evening of the reading, it was impossible to determine where the event would take place. There were no posters, and no one to whom we spoke knew anything about a poetry reading. We wandered into a building where we found several black-robed dons filing into a small library, and caused a brief stir when our scruffy group joined them. Altogether, there were no more than twenty people in the room when Lowell appeared. Not a single student from the university was in attendance, and I realized that that was how these dons had arranged it. "Blue-nosed bastards," Theodore Roethke had called the British.

Lowell read for only thirty minutes or so; then the don who'd introduced him asked for questions. A stubborn silence oppressed the room. I began to grow uncomfortable as the seconds ticked by, a minute now, and thought Lowell grew uncomfortable as well. It seemed we had all been plunged underwater. No one in the room was breathing, and I sensed a stony animosity on the part of the faculty. Was *this* the best America had to offer? Finally I could no longer bear the tension. I raised my hand, then blurted out some question about confessional poetry. Before Lowell could respond, even before he could have registered the question, the don began railing at me, suggesting that my question had insulted Lowell who certainly did not write confessional poetry, and—he went on—if *that* was the kind of question that could be expected, then there would be no more questions! I was mortified. No one moved. Except Lowell.

"If there will be no more questions," he arched an eyebrow at the don, "I'd like to read one more poem." He turned toward me. "It's a confessional poem." Then Robert Lowell recited "Skunk Hour" to the few feverish American students who sat among those blue-nosed bastards.

The Soul

Recently, on the way to the outpatient facility to have the fluid clogging one ear siphoned, I saw my neighbor fiercely beckoning, so pulled into his driveway. He knew that I was heading to the hospital and, a religious man, asked if he might pray for me. What harm? But he took me by surprise when he knelt on the macadam, a penitent among gardening tools, and rested his brow on my forearm while I remained seated in the idling car. Blink-182 thrashed on the FM, suddenly loud enough to warp the speakers, so he urged his voice upward past my good left ear. *Let Michael return from the hospital able to hear again, Lord*, he pleaded. *Let him receive Your bounty.* He couldn't stop himself: *Lead him into Your fold before Judgment.*

Who understands the whimsies of rural reception, much less the vicissitudes of God? I have a colleague who asked my creative writing students if they thought I was going to hell. *Waters? On skis*, one laughed, and when they told me, I reminded them that "skiing" might be the only word in the English language to employ the double *i*. *Hawaii*, one said. *English*, I repeated, racing downhill, the slope all to myself.

III

THE TETHER

Miles-deep rents in the floor's
gritty fabric where water
spews into water—a primal
violence at the earth's core—

attract the alien, light-
leaking fistulae and pods
that ascend and fall, ascend
and fall, misshapen aspirants

assuming endless pilgrimage.
The bubbling faults beckon them
forth. And the marine
biologist hunkered in metal,

the uterine bathysphere,
gazes open-mouthed
when the surface generator
triggers the lamps to reveal

such impossible yearning:
God's disinherited, the nameless
flaws who have so much farther
to climb, their mute kingdom

allowing its immense blackness
to conceal His cold
fumblings, furious gestures,
as if we might begin again

among these divine zeroes,
these creaturely scraps
mimicking grace, these
nightmarish drafts of flesh,

these never-to-be-called.
Some almost-shape drifts by.
Awe. A distant knocking.
—Then the long haul.

DEEP-SEA SPONGE

Venus's Flower Basket
Euplectella aspergillum

All froth & spiral & vast interior architectural
    complexity, this latticework skeleton
        beckons shrimp in their fierce but spindly
throes of seasonal mating, twenty-legged
    couples who cross the thousand
        thresholds, small enough to be housed
in such spicular domesticity, but who then grow
    too large to leave, remaining forever
        paradisiacal lovers, or bitter
cagelings undone by Darwinian trickery—
    unlike maggots, which seethe with festivity,
        each grub inside a skull an individual
brain cell engorged with furious speculation
    regarding its final destination.
        Within either cathedral's rich brocade,
worm or prawn labors to return
    ritual to pagan roots—gluttony & lust—
        while we who found the sponge, under less
pressure, wing it back to our suburban home
    to decorate a hutch, to remind each other
        how we survive, and why we love.

SCARABS

Coleoptera scarabaeidae
. . . their representations used in ancient Egypt as symbols of resurrection

Red dirt pummeled by goat-herd generations
plumes the path bearing our sandal soles' impress
till rain feathers flat each warped hourglass.

And who are we?—twin nobodies
unsung in the untranslatable sagas,
abandoned in the ongoing odysseys.

Vipers tongue our noon-stunted shades.
Like savage forebears, we dwell upon the dirt
where beetles, green-black glints, each a mini-

Sisyphus, commence their crucial business:
turning the earth so that torrents of light
sweep vast provinces into the future . . .

where, palsied and riven by syphilis,
we no longer recognize our ravaged
faces, or recall lush gardens of our making.

How will I find you once I awaken,
crawling from caverns, blinded by sun,
naked amid the alien thistle,

no longer speaking our common tongue?—
while dazzling drudges, jeweled citizens,
tumble forward their terrible burdens,

rotating newly-formed planets of dung.

PROCESSIONAL

One stacks her cells
in the spiral
staircase of an empty snail-shell
writes J. Henri Fabre
regarding bees
in one rhapsodic essay
praising *my dear insects*
for such resourcefulness,
but on January 30, 1896,
in his famous but cruel
textbook experiment,
he rearranged the scent
that marked the trail
assumed by a single,
unwavering line
of the common
caterpillar
who *spins his great purses*
in pine branches,
their path now circular,
so these stubborn
leaf-foragers
traveled for hours,
then days, spooling miles
till exhausting themselves,
finally starving—
all to the wonder
of their rational recorder
who possessed even less
sympathy for humans,
sketching in his journal
the virgin's bower

(*Clematis vitalba*),
the famous beggar's herb
which reddens the skin
and produces the sores
in request among
our sham cripples.

COMMERCE

Niagara Falls
18—

Some half-wit Barnum, amateur Noah,
fashioned an ark—a salvaged, broken barge—
to populate with creatures trapped or bought:
black bear, wolverine, a fox like a flame,

peacocks, possum, hogs, raccoon, wailing tribe
of forsaken dogs, weasel, skunk, even—
according to eyewitness reports—six
silver monkeys shipped by rail from New York,

God's mange-thumbed menagerie chained to planks
that would have floated three runaway slaves
had not abolitionists threatened court.
Then Noah bid his bestiary goodbye,

the raft of lamentation set adrift,
its creatures more confused than crazed, almost
calm as the ark spiraled toward the maelstrom,
the waters' vast uproar drowning weak cries,

white mists like shrouds enveloping the crew
while spectators whooped and scrambled both banks
and newsboys shilled beer a nickel a glass
till it perched midair on the precipice. . . .

Folklore swears the bear survived, pummeled ashore
where men beat her with clubs and muzzled her,
then dragged that rough beast saloon to saloon
where drafts of whiskey were chugged down her throat.

By morning she lay a rank heap on State—
schoolchildren leapfrogged the raggedy corpse.
Then one cat was found, eyeless, legs broken,
so for the next decade tramps tortured strays

to sell them to tourists, farm boys, and Poles
as The Cat Swept Over Niagara Falls,
singular souvenir, His living hand,
New World miracle—only one dollar.

2 REVELATION 1:2

—six human subjects
                    dying
each on a bed on a platform beam scale
each monitored for loss of urine
                              loss
of air from lungs, evaporation of moisture
due to death-sweat, due to fear—

death of 1st patient: the beam drops
and does not bounce back
                         recording
the loss of three-fourths of an ounce

2nd patient: a sudden drop at the exact
moment of death: one and one-half ounces

3rd patient: 4th patient: et cetera

Dr. Duncan MacDougall of Haverhill, MA
after observing all six deaths
concluded that a loss of substance
not accounted for by "known channels"
occurs at death, hence

"Hypothesis Concerning Soul Substance
Together with Experimental Evidence
of the Existence of Such Substance":
American Medicine II (4) :240-43 (April 1907)

Cassius: . . . *raven, crows and kites,*
Fly o'er our heads and downward look on us,
As we were sickly prey: their shadows seem
A canopy most fatal . . .
—Julius Caesar V, I

WHO ARE THESE RAVENS

smudging each window?— insisting their kind
  upon bare branches, hauling behind them
    the terrible dawn, then spattering it

  with the ragged, monotonous calligraphy
    of their hundred hewn and inky bodies?
      The sentences they inscribe remain unread

    like haiku thrust upon you by Buddhist friends,
      or novels scavenged from boxes at yard sales,
        only to be boxed then sold again.

    So the ravens resound their brief histories,
      where they're going and where they've been,
        scritch by *scritch* on rice paper air,

      assuming authority through hinged soliloquies,
        yet never communing their corvine despair.
          Instead, like the dead with whom they share

  common anonymity, they focus their raucous
    energy toward a central core—
      stone-dense, like a fossilized egg—

till they burst suddenly heavenward,
   almost familiar, no longer an unkindness
      but a face now, one recognizable

god whose blackness so terrifies
   that you turn away, or turn inward—
      to pray, to admonish the soul.

OSSUARY

Kutna Hora
Czech Republic

Coat of arms, spidery chandelier, sui
generis baptismal font, even these
altars propping now-vacant monstrances
were crafted of bones by a half-blind monk,
architect of the anonymous dead,
who cleansed then whitewashed skulls & vertebrae
once the plague had blazed through Moravia,
who stooped to stack & interlock femurs,
clavicles, ilia, et cetera. . . .
One bored daytripper blasts Radiohead
from her slung Sony while giggling classmates
trigger alarms in their desire to touch
such scrubbed evidence of mortality,
to finger hollow sockets of distant
forebears jigsawed together in cool vaults.
Radiohead segues into U2.
The widow hawking postcards hustles us
toward sunlight—we've breathed centuries enough
of mold & spore & crumbling fibulae.
We've witnessed enough. These schoolgirls want more.
Let them follow each other—a scraggly
crusade of backpacks & pierced lips & brows—
till they flame to spirit down the noon glare.
Let us all unburden ourselves before
the next plague, the next manic devotions,
before the coming of next year's rock gods,
the rending of the bones of the middle
ear, before the puzzle's final fragment
locks into place, before wind, before fire.

THE CRUSADES

The Cloisters
1998

Bone Thugs-n-Harmony trip-hop the Sony
   balanced on the pocked stone
shield of the sarcophagus, c. 1248.
   Neither Jean D'Alluye's open
eyes nor lion crouching at his feet
   registers surprise, though one
guard warns the schoolboys, who
   snicker into the courtyard to smoke.
We clasp hands among these medieval
   curiosities, the shimmering
tapestries & Books of Hours, ornate
   reliquaries that once preserved
a bone from the foot of St. Anne
   or splinter of the True Cross.
Bass-throbs echo through the vaults
   as the Fort Tryon citizenry
mourn the glory lost in the martyrdom
   of the Notorious B.I.G.

BACKRUB

"There is no exquisite beauty without some strangeness in the proportion."
—Poe, quoting Bacon, in "Ligeia"

Her pale & plum-splotched skin
hung in voluminous folds like stained bedsheets,
like the hand-me-down habit of an unchaste nun.

Famous on campus, she resembled in her wrappings
a wet dream by Christo, a draped tornado
clanging its ceramics, her bracelets & earrings,

warning the unwary in her path. . . . Sometimes
she squatted in stairwells near mailboxes,
immense storybook toad, beckoning

passersby with a wheedling tongue,
wanting someone *please* to touch her, anyone
who wouldn't think twice before scratching

a flea-bitten mongrel behind its torn ear,
who wouldn't recoil from her simple request.
So one morning, why not, I volunteered.

I trailed in her wake to her room
where she'd tacked sketches onto walls, inked
genitalia eyed & winged, where she shrugged

her blouse coil by coil up her back & off, then lay
facedown on the narrow bed, ample fleshfolds
almost sweeping the floor, & after several moments'

hesitation, after staring down that mound of clay,
I began to work its heaped convolutions,
fingertips deepening in the plush

ripples, the yeasty, never-to-be exuviae,
scoring the soundtrack of her sighs & gurgles,
immersing my whole being in the ceaseless kneading

till I could no longer tell where my knuckles
dissolved & her thunderous billows began,
losing myself in the laborious process of creation.

IV

MAKING LOVE AT THE FROST PLACE

Franconia, NH

His name—**R. Frost**—writ large in bold strokes on the mailbox,
the village luminary
hunkers in wraithlike presence over his writing desk,
or shuffles in slippers past
the open hearth, milky hair and graphite-needled face
such familiar portraiture
we can't not see him rage as we clutch each other, not
hear him groan as we commence
late August lovemaking during such perishable
tenancy, until we learn
again, *night falling fast*, what schoolchildren flame to know:
the common language that breathes
autumn into *apples*, winter into *sleep* and *snow*.

ISAMU NOGUCHI

1904–1988

". . . known to his Indiana high school class as Sam Gilmour"
—Artforum

Jasper, serpentine, red Persian travertine,
   Languedoc marble—Noguchi
      must have yearned to hear the names
     clasped in stone, the whispering
within the glacial strata, the icy vestibules,

who could view in each crumbly fragment
   of scarp, each pinched swamp-flake,
      the miniature comets and bursting
     swirls like time-trapped sperm
and fossilized egg—his brilliant, briny

ancestors struggling to create something new:
   not Sam, but some other "continuously
      expatriated person" who gauges
     the distance between himself and the world,
between "I" and "you," then chisels a door

for the one locked without. Or within: *Isamu.*

JUNKIE TEMPO

"You know what it is? It's a junkie tempo."
—Quincy Jones on Miles Davis's *Kind of Blue*

Not monkey time, not pony time,
not night time is the right time,
not if you've got the place I've got the time,
not even a time for every purpose under heaven, no,

but almost—not quite—time after time
once Miles had summoned it into his body,
then wrenched each blue note loose to be transformed
through the blackness compressed inside his horn,

his standard now, his signature,
his Montreux-with-Q
blowing-back-to-the-day time: 52nd Street time,
Birdland time, 5 Spot time, Plugged Nickel time,

always time and time again relentless time:
time, Miles used to smile, like a motherfucker.

SONNET FOR STRUMMER

1952–2002

"Where ignorant armies clash by night"
—Matthew Arnold, "Dover Beach"

One less spiked art school burnout on the dole,
you let your name bestow occupation,
then thrashed the racism of Thatcher's nation,
spunk and outrage trebling rock'n'roll
that jabbed island reggae with safety pins,
pricked politics with a fat spliff of soul.

Patois and curses
                    Vinegar and piss
All her former colonies have spoken
London's
            burning   DA   No longer exists
the King's English
                        or safe European
                                    home

66

BALTHUS

When the angel arrived, bare-breasted, androgynous,
its lower half sheathed in tulle
bluer than the plums in ceramic bowls propped on stools,
the vetch in the studio
revived; colors assumed blunt authority; even
yellow became heavy. Bells
tolled from tinny speakers: Mozart striking precise notes
with an almost disarming
simplicity, their grace and gravity suggesting
the long marriage of pleasure
and sorrow. *Così fan tutte*. I named the angel
Katia, thus assigning
gender. Now each brushstroke resonates with tumescence.
Black mirror, red table, moth,
white skirt. *Nude in Front of a Mantel. Girl on Her Knees.*
Sprawled on a chair, Katia
pretends to read a volume of sonnets by Rilke.
I pencil in my journal:
To assume God's face, to ponder what He incarnates:
landscape, young girls' flesh, newly
ripe spring fruits, trees full of sap, the sweetness of sleeping
children. I know that this work—
a painter's required labor—always means redemption.
When I look up, the angel
has fallen asleep, but the plums, those black plums bursting
flecked skins, have been devoured.

PAVESE

Cesare Pavese (b. 1908) committed suicide on August 27, 1950. His rela-
tionship with American actress Constance Dowling had ended. Nine days
earlier he had written the final entry in his diary: "I will not write anymore."

I inhabit this body, Don Niccolo de' Pelagati,
as you inhabited for weeks the iron cage
suspended above the filthy streets of Ferrara, 1495.
Birds convened their solemn judiciary.
Once you snared a pigeon by its talon,
then ate it still living, morsel by feathery morsel,
its frantic heart pumping blood into your mouth.
The merciless sun seared your skin,
each blister a tiny Vatican.
At night the northern wind whipped you with its icy lash.
When you died, one yellow eye
spilled onto the street; your flesh rotted to rags.
Still you swayed above commerce and pageantry,
raining lightly onto cobblestones:
a shriveled ear, a shrunken thumb, what remained of your sex
puddling below for rats to tongue.
I suffer this body, forefather, doubter,
as your living body and unregenerate corpse
suffered its iron cage.
Already I have become one of the old men
who endures each day without love.
Non scriverò piú.
I rage in your remnants and stains.

LA BOHÈME: THE NEW ENGLAND MARIONETTES

Peterborough, NH

Rodolfo rubs clay hands against the cold,
   then tosses his work-in-progress into the fire.
      Better to survive the Parisian winter
        than allow the soul a sheen of ice
   that further diminishes its muffled voice.

When Mimi floats across the garret, clutching
   one unlit candle, Rodolfo basks in sudden
      warmth, gazes into her daubed eyes
        to recognize the promise of spring
   kept alive through ceaseless embroidering.

Their duet ("O soave fanciulla!") proclaims newfound
   love, but three acts later Mimi will die
      as Rodolfo shouts her name across rooftops.
        What could the bohemians have done
   but hock heavy coats, pawn earrings for medicine?

The grief in Pavarotti's throat, the enormous skulls
   weighing each marionette, strain toward the bridge
      where, cloaked in black, the almost-
        invisible masters allow strings
   to fall slack, then cradle their stars in aching

arms before slipping the lovers into chamois sacks.
   We all drink at the nearby inn while
      Rodolfo and Mimi lie inches apart,
        unable to touch, or rekindle the wick,
   while the puppeteers feel the Scotch's fire

roar through their souls: one century gone, Puccini
   gone, Pavese gone by his own hand, in Turin,
      where the opera was first performed,
         before art gave over its grief
      to the gestures of little people made of clay.

RAYMOND CARVER

5 A.M.: he slippers downstairs for coffee, one joint,
some rest after not sleeping
again, not drinking, after phone calls & late night talk:
the colleague whose petition
for promotion cited his reading *The New York Times*
"on a daily basis," then
listed prestigious journals that had rejected work.
Jeez, Ray had grinned, head shaking.
The dog scratches itself up off the wooden floor, cocks
its head at this soft touch, this
gentle goofball, whines *out?*—so Ray props open the door
for this mutt who has never
been outside without its chain, who pads onto the porch
fronting our busy street, turns
back just as Ray lets the screen door shut, then slowly slinks
off to some great adventure.
Hours later, I'm jogging the block, jingling an empty
leash, shouting "Bobby?" while Ray
crisscrosses the neighborhood in his cramped Volkswagen.
Did we find the dog? Of course—
it leapt onto his front seat, then panted home to sprawl
belly-up by the fireplace,
legs flung open in some canine parody of bliss.
In 1979
Bobby was still alive, Ray was still alive, my wife
slept through that particular
commotion, we all ate breakfast in the sunny nook
while the days ahead gathered

into "gravy," Ray called them, into poems & stories . . .
& Ray sits at the table,
laughing again, shaking his head, *Can you believe it?*
Jeez, what was that guy thinking?

                                   1938–1988

72

ELEGANT LADY

in memoriam Mary Gay Calcott

". . . quiet and pure as / a peach"
—Adam Zagajewski

His mother loved all the flesh-colored fruits,
   mandarins, peaches, the green-going-to-yellow
      Gloria Mundi and Star in the East apples,

so she would heap them in baskets on the table
   where sunsets dazzling the window
      burnished pale skins, kindling low fires

that warmed the boy as he reckoned his sums.
   He was puzzling the multiplication tables
      when his mother marked her Daphne du Maurier.

Seven times eight was always hardest,
   so she peeled oranges, thumbing apart
      their pulpy crescents, then split

three peaches into wedges, until
   fifty-six parentheses of fruit
      arrayed the polished tabletop.

How could he forget the answer now?
   That evening they jumbled together a salad
      and, grinning, ate the boy's homework.

Tonight he fills several creamware bowls
   to attract the waning light. Quince, apples,
      fat Bosc pears, peaches flushed yellow. . . .

When he bites the one named Elegant Lady,
   sweet rills furrow fleshy lips. *Fifty-six.*
      She loved the peaches so.

BLUE ANKLE

That stooped old woman who tremors through Kieślowski's films
takes almost an hour, it seems,
to heft one milk carton into the recycling bin,
groaning her arm up only
so high so long, failing again to push the plastic
through the rubber-flanged circle
of the public receptacle.
                              And the young woman's
always watching. Should she leave
the window to help the woman slip the container
into the drop or flutter
her letter—in another sequence, another film—
toward the narrow mailbox slot?
One friend half-jokes that we're all coming to a bad end.
Is the arthritic woman
some future version of herself, blue ankle swollen,
spine hunched like a question mark,
drab woolen coat too thin to repel the frost-edged wind,
scarf askew, the few whiskers
poking from her chin like the black spikes of sea urchins?
And after she releases,
at last, the empty jug into the receptacle,
where does she go?—to which cramped
studio along which pocked lane where art school dropouts
loiter, racing engines, sleek
cycles propped on the sidewalk so she's forced to weave through
a labyrinth of chrome and fumes
to reach her door, then ascend steep steps to the fifth floor?
Mercifully, Kieślowski's
camera doesn't accompany her.
                              Nor have we seen
one of those boys, as a joke,

not meaning to hit her, lob a loose cobble, striking
the woman's ankle so fire
sears up her leg, but she drags her foot forward without
turning, the boys dumbfounded,
embarrassed now, till the one who tossed the stone, almost
as an afterthought, shouts "Jew!"—
then the rest scoop up fistfuls of rubble and warn her
to keep moving, though no one
tosses another stone, and the woman feels too much
pain to allow consciousness
its thorny, inexhaustible registry of fear.
All coming to a bad end. . . .
Dominika turns from snow-struck glass back to her room
where her lover smokes in bed.
He seems vain, superfluous now, though she once enjoyed
encircling his waist, pressing
her cheek against the cold black leather of his jacket
that smelled of gas and absinthe
while the cycle surged Warsaw's crooked passageways, once
took pleasure in their vulgar
colleagues who preened, crowlike, uncircumcised cocks erect,
as she sketched them for art class.
Her mother's dead ten years. Her father's letters bear stamps
from a distant country, so
this boy's the only one who holds her these days, these nights
all coming to a bad end
though later she will dream the woman rinsing one dish
or watching soap operas fling
vertical corpses across blank windows while she soothes
her bruised ankle with chipped ice,
with a gentleness no lover has ever possessed.

GREEN SWEATER

Playa del Carmen
Quintana Roo

Subtle gradations of horizontal
  strata ink toward shore,
    the dissipating squall
  erasing even the gray-green
waters precisely the shade
  of my sweater, the *exact*
    shade—didn't the Mayan
  waitress tell me last night?—
of my eyes. Shopkeepers lower
  shutters against the lashing
    rains, sequence
  after sequence needling the reef
like guitar-thrash broadcast
  from an offshore pirate
    station; even the barflies
  smashed to their visors on Cuba
libres shuffle into the Sandbox's
  dank interior . . . but this sweater:
    after the service
  my mother asked me to choose
among his belongings spread like booty
  on their bed: Rolexes, Olympic
    commemorative pins, one
  hundred silver, jade, onyx
and turquoise rings, a jewelry-box
  like a lost sea chest stashed
    with loot, but still
  too numb to desire anything
(yet wanting to please her), I cast

about the room to find it tossed
   across the wing of a chair:
     "Suppose I take that sweater?"
I'm wearing it now while tenacious,
   topless Germans wade through
     sea-spinach the storm's
   gathered, lifting sun-splotched
legs among torn leaves, the sea's
   glittering, stable currency, ungainly
     creatures enacting charade:
heron earth as it is in Heron.
How falsely we approximate nature, lacking
   modesty. How flirtatious
     that waitress in her flattery
   toward some hefty tip, though
I'm back for her grin, wrapped again
   in my father's punctured pullover—
     husk-thin, misshapen, but
   reliable on this jutting wedge
of Mexico where tipsy tourists limbo.
   I've never seen the sea this particular
     shade of green, I'd tell him
   if he could be here, nursing
a Dos Equis ("Two horses!" I heard one
   collegian bray) in the storm-cooled
     air. Then: *Dad,*
   do you recognize this sweater?
The waters begin again to assume
   their charged, heavenly colors,
     colors we approximate,
   lacking modesty, here on earth. . . .
Green soothes the soul. Lost father,
   abiding spirit, generative
     calm: *I've never felt*
   so loved so far from home.

TZADDIKIM NISTARIM

—(Hebrew): the thirty-six unknown men in each
generation who keep the world from falling apart

Brain-damaged, the residents shriek like crows in the pure
pleasure of recognizing
each other as they tug us into *Bricolage Arts*.
Here is a cardboard tube smeared
red, studded with papier-mâché O-mouthed angel heads.
Here is a wooden matchstick
schooner rowed by creatures winged with wire who angle
their bent craft toward safe harbor.

In the chapel, our rapt guide
prays as he was taught: palms smashed together, thumbtips pressed
to lower lip in the hope
that whispered amens might ski down that fleshy slope, then
shoot like fireworks toward Heaven.
Years ago, my grandmother recited her seven
names for G-d—*Yod Heh Vav Heh*
Yeshua   Yahweh   Elohim   Hashem   El-Shaddai . . .
I can't remember them all,
but grew fervent in their whirling, each groaned syllable
bracing my desperate faith.

One woman with Down's syndrome
grasps my wrist and sweeps my cheek with water and blue dust
seeping from her chalkboard sponge.
A mark upon us both now, we ghost into the crowd—
some few souls bearing inky
webbing, strange ciphers; others tattooed invisibly,
unable to recognize

one another, though even in their simple gestures—
buying a bird-shaped terra
cotta whistle or crooked wax candle—they save us.

THE BOOK OF CONSTELLATIONS

Dominican Republic

We'd forgotten, again, *The Book of Constellations*,
so stretched on sand, unable
to finger even one winter warrior, to sketch one
creature lumbering shaggily
past muted heroes assembled star by star by God.
Or by man who squints below,
imposing myth in fearful murk upon far heavens.
No brilliance here. One hand stalks
crabwise into yours as husked coconuts plunge earthward.
We attempt slight revisions:
naming constellations after less mythical beings
who ruined our half-century
by harming helpless creatures left briefly in their charge:
Idi Amin, Ceaușescu,
Marcos, Pinochet, the Papa Docs and Baby Docs,
that hypocritical fool
Strom Thurmond dragged to hell fifty-three years past his time,
Pope John Paul—but then we stop.
When did human love mutate into this reptilian
seething that makes us despise
ourselves? *Whose hand in mine?* So we revise: Noguchi,
Miles, Allen Ginsberg, Balthus,
Joe Strummer, Raymond Carver, Muriel Rukeyser,
Bob Marley and Audre Lorde!—
heroic trespassers thrumming heaven's negative
spaces, prodding the icy
stars to wheel once more and assume fierce grandeur with each
invocation of their names,
who kindle such generative, indelible fires

across the universe, *yes,*
our only universe, dear God, beloved, amen.

NOTES

"Fauns Fleeing Before an Automobile": Beneš Knüpfer, oil on canvas, 1905, Museum of Modern Art, Prague.

"Poinciana": a tropical tree bearing orange and red blossoms. Also the title of the influential jazz recording released in 1951 by pianist Ahmad Jamal.

"Erotic Roman Antiquities": lines 8–10 from an article by Nicholas Fox Weber, *The New York Times*, August 13, 2000.

"Miserere": the first word in the Vulgate text of Psalm 51: also the score for unaccompanied chorus (1981) by Polish composer Henryk Górecki (b. 1933). His text consists of only five words: "Domine Deus noster, Miserere nobis": *Lord our God, have mercy on us.* "Für Alina": secular piece (1976) by Estonian composer Arvo Pärt (b. 1935), whose own "Miserere" was scored in 1989.

"What•ev•er": St. Teresa quoted in *Teresa of Avila: The Progress of a Soul* by Cathleen Medwick (Knopf, 1999).

"Deep-Sea Sponge": adapted, in part, from an article in *The New York Times*, January 31, 2005.

"Processional": Fabre's experiment with Pine Processional caterpillars (*Thaumatopoeidae processionea*) from *The Insect World of J. Henri Fabre* (Beacon Press, 1991).

"2 Revelation 1:2": MacDougall's experiment recounted in *Stiff: The Curious Lives of Human Cadavers* by Mary Roach (Norton, 2003) and in *The Daily Times* (Salisbury, MD), July 11, 2003.

"The Crusades": rap artist Christopher Wallace *aka* Biggie Smalls *aka* Notorious B.I.G. murdered on March 9, 1997.

"Making Love at the Frost Place": *for Mihaela*: with gratitude to Jeffrey Skinner, 1997 poet-in-residence, for the invitation.

"Junkie Tempo": *in memoriam Miles Davis, d. September 28, 1991*: Quincy Jones ("Q") quoted in *Kind of Blue: The Making of the Miles Davis Masterpiece* by Ashley Kahn (Da Capo Press, 2000). Jazz purists objected to Miles' recording of the pop tune "Time After Time" (words and music by Cyndi Lauper and Rob Hyman) on his 1984 release *You're Under Arrest*. Miles last played Montreux on July 8, 1991.

"Sonnet for Strummer": *in memoriam Joe Strummer, d. December 22, 2002*: founding member of The Clash, seminal British punk band.

"Balthus": *in memoriam Balthasar Klossowski, d. February 18, 2001*: the italicized lines appear, in slightly different form, in his memoir, *Vanished Splendors*, as told to Alaín Vircondelet, translated by Benjamin Ivry (Ecco, 2002). Several other lines are drawn from this source.

"Pavese": Don Niccolo de' Pelagati was locked in an iron cage outside the tower of San Giuliano on August 12. A priest, he had committed numerous crimes, including murder.

"Elegant Lady": with a nod to Wayne Dodd.

"Blue Ankle": *in memoriam Krzysztof Kieślowski, d. March 13, 1996*: Polish filmmaker whose films include *Decalogue*, *The Double Life of Veronique*, and *Three Colors: Blue, White, Red*. Triggered by a recurring scene, the poem does not focus on any single film.

ACKNOWLEDGMENTS

Grateful acknowledgment is made to the editors of journals and anthologies in which these poems, often in earlier versions, appeared:

Arts & Letters: "Deep-Sea Sponge," "Tzaddikim Nistarim";

Connecticut Review: "Blue Ankle," "Green Sweater";

Crab Orchard Review: "Sonnet for Strummer";

Crazyhorse: "The Tether";

The English Record: "The Crusades," "Elegant Lady";

FIELD: "Balthus";

5 A.M.: "Poinciana," "The Book of Constellations";

The Gettysburg Review: "Fauns Fleeing Before an Automobile," "Commerce";

The Kenyon Review: "Miserere," "Erotic Roman Antiquities," "Wedding Dress";

Kestrel: "Who Are These Ravens";

Near East Review: "*A Note on the Poems,*" "Junkie Tempo";

New Letters: "The Bicycle and the Soul," "Pavese";

One Trick Pony: "Family Outing";

Poetry: "Black Olives";

RUNES: "Making Love at the Frost Place," "Raymond Carver";

Salt Hill Journal: "Isamu Noguchi";

Shenandoah: "Scarabs";

The Southern Review: "American Eel," "What•ev•er," "Backrub";

Sycamore Review: "Eddie's Parrot";

TriQuarterly: "Bosporus," "Processional," "2 Revelation 1:2";

West Branch: "Ossuary," "*La Bohème*: The New England Marionettes."

"The Tether" was reprinted in a limited-edition letterpress pamphlet, *Naked Sea Butterflies* (Red Dragonfly Press, 2001). Special thanks to Scott King.

"Commerce" was reprinted in *Anglophonia: French Journal of English Studies, The Pushcart Prize XXVIII: Best of the Small Presses*, ed. Bill Henderson (Pushcart Press, 2004), and *The Pushcart Book of Poetry*, ed. Joan Murray (Pushcart Press, 2006).

"Miserere" was reprinted in *Wild and Whirling Words: A Poetic Conversation*, ed. H. L. Hix (Etruscan Press, 2004).

"Black Olives" was reprinted in *Kindled Terraces: American Poets in Greece*, ed. Don Schofield (Truman State UP, 2004) and *O Taste and See*, eds. David Lee Garrison and Terry Hermsen (Bottom Dog Press, 2003).

"Making Love at the Frost Place" was reprinted in *Visiting Frost: Poems Inspired by the Life and Work of Robert Frost*, eds. Thom Tammaro and Sheila Coghill (U of Iowa P, 2005) and *Chance of a Ghost*, eds. Philip Miller and Gloria Vando (Helicon Nine Editions, 2005).

"Wedding Dress" and "Blue Ankle" were reprinted in *Poetry Calendar 2006* and *Poetry Calendar 2007*, respectively, ed. Shafiq Naz (Alhambra, 2005 and 2006).

"Wedding Dress," "Miserere," "Erotic Roman Antiquities," and "Poinciana" were reprinted in the limited-edition *Signature Series* for the Catskill Poetry Workshop at Hartwick College.

Several poems were reprinted on-line in *Enskyment* and *Caught in the Net* (England). Special thanks to Dan Masterson.

Carol Frost, Robert Hedin, Dave Smith, and Elizabeth Spires offered suggestions toward the revision of several poems. I remain fortunate in friendship.

I remain grateful to Laure-Anne Bosselaar and Kurt Brown for time at Carpe Diem in Provence in 2001, and to the Ledig-Rowohlt Foundation for a residency at Le Château de Lavigny in Switzerland in 2005.

Gratitude also to the Maryland State Arts Council for Individual Artist Awards, to Timothy O'Rourke of the Fulton School at Salisbury University for release time, and to Shara McCallum, Director of the Stadler Center for Poetry at Bucknell University, for the 2005 residency that provided me time to complete this book.

ABOUT THE AUTHOR

Michael Waters is Professor of English at Salisbury University on the Eastern Shore of Maryland and teaches in the New England College MFA Program in Poetry. The recipient of a Fellowship in Creative Writing from the National Endowment for the Arts, Individual Artist Awards from the Maryland State Arts Council, and three Pushcart Prizes, he has taught in Creative Writing Programs at Ohio University and the University of Maryland, and has been Visiting Professor of American Literature at the University of Athens, Greece, as well as Banister Writer-in-Residence at Sweet Briar College, Stadler Poet-in-Residence at Bucknell University, and Distinguished Poet-in-Residence at Wichita State University.

BOA Editions, Ltd.:
American Poets Continuum Series

No. 1   *The Fuhrer Bunker: A Cycle of Poems in Progress*
W. D. Snodgrass

No. 2   *She*
M. L. Rosenthal

No. 3   *Living With Distance*
Ralph J. Mills, Jr.

No. 4   *Not Just Any Death*
Michael Waters

No. 5   *That Was Then: New and Selected Poems*
Isabella Gardner

No. 6   *Things That Happen Where There Aren't Any People*
William Stafford

No. 7   *The Bridge of Change: Poems 1974–1980*
John Logan

No. 8   *Signatures*
Joseph Stroud

No. 9   *People Live Here: Selected Poems 1949–1983*
Louis Simpson

No. 10   *Yin*
Carolyn Kizer

No. 11   *Duhamel: Ideas of Order in Little Canada*
Bill Tremblay

No. 12   *Seeing It Was So*
Anthony Piccione

No. 13   *Hyam Plutzik: The Collected Poems*

No. 14   *Good Woman: Poems and a Memoir 1969–1980*
Lucille Clifton

No. 15   *Next: New Poems*
Lucille Clifton

No. 16   *Roxa: Voices of the Culver Family*
William B. Patrick

No. 17   *John Logan: The Collected Poems*

No. 18   *Isabella Gardner: The Collected Poems*

No. 19   *The Sunken Lightship*
Peter Makuck

No. 20   *The City in Which I Love You*
Li-Young Lee

No. 21   *Quilting: Poems 1987–1990*
Lucille Clifton

No. 22   *John Logan: The Collected Fiction*

No. 23   *Shenandoah and Other Verse Plays*
Delmore Schwartz

No. 24   *Nobody Lives on Arthur Godfrey Boulevard*
Gerald Costanzo

No. 25   *The Book of Names: New and Selected Poems*
Barton Sutter

No. 26   *Each in His Season*
W. D. Snodgrass

No. 27   *Wordworks: Poems Selected and New*
Richard Kostelanetz

No. 28   *What We Carry*
Dorianne Laux

No. 29 *Red Suitcase*
Naomi Shihab Nye

No. 30 *Song*
Brigit Pegeen Kelly

No. 31 *The Fuehrer Bunker:*
The Complete Cycle
W. D. Snodgrass

No. 32 *For the Kingdom*
Anthony Piccione

No. 33 *The Quicken Tree*
Bill Knott

No. 34 *These Upraised Hands*
William B. Patrick

No. 35 *Crazy Horse in Stillness*
William Heyen

No. 36 *Quick, Now, Always*
Mark Irwin

No. 37 *I Have Tasted the Apple*
Mary Crow

No. 38 *The Terrible Stories*
Lucille Clifton

No. 39 *The Heat of Arrivals*
Ray Gonzalez

No. 40 *Jimmy & Rita*
Kim Addonizio

No. 41 *Green Ash, Red Maple,*
Black Gum
Michael Waters

No. 42 *Against Distance*
Peter Makuck

No. 43 *The Night Path*
Laurie Kutchins

No. 44 *Radiography*
Bruce Bond

No. 45 *At My Ease: Uncollected Poems*
of the Fifties and Sixties
David Ignatow

No. 46 *Trillium*
Richard Foerster

No. 47 *Fuel*
Naomi Shihab Nye

No. 48 *Gratitude*
Sam Hamill

No. 49 *Diana, Charles, & the Queen*
William Heyen

No. 50 *Plus Shipping*
Bob Hicok

No. 51 *Cabato Sentora*
Ray Gonzalez

No. 52 *We Didn't Come Here for This*
William B. Patrick

No. 53 *The Vandals*
Alan Michael Parker

No. 54 *To Get Here*
Wendy Mnookin

No. 55 *Living Is What I Wanted:*
Last Poems
David Ignatow

No. 56 *Dusty Angel*
Michael Blumenthal

No. 57 *The Tiger Iris*
Joan Swift

No. 58 *White City*
Mark Irwin

No. 59 *Laugh at the End of the World:*
Collected Comic Poems
1969–1999
Bill Knott

No. 60 *Blessing the Boats: New and*
Selected Poems: 1988–2000
Lucille Clifton

No. 61 *Tell Me*
Kim Addonizio

No. 62 *Smoke*
Dorianne Laux

No. 63 *Parthenopi: New and Selected Poems*
Michael Waters

No. 64 *Rancho Notorious*
Richard Garcia

No. 65 *Jam*
Joe-Anne McLaughlin

No. 66 *A. Poulin, Jr. Selected Poems*
Edited, with an Introduction by Michael Waters

No. 67 *Small Gods of Grief*
Laure-Anne Bosselaar

No. 68 *Book of My Nights*
Li-Young Lee

No. 69 *Tulip Farms and Leper Colonies*
Charles Harper Webb

No. 70 *Double Going*
Richard Foerster

No. 71 *What He Took*
Wendy Mnookin

No. 72 *The Hawk Temple at Tierra Grande*
Ray Gonzalez

No. 73 *Mules of Love*
Ellen Bass

No. 74 *The Guests at the Gate*
Anthony Piccione

No. 75 *Dumb Luck*
Sam Hamill

No. 76 *Love Song with Motor Vehicles*
Alan Michael Parker

No. 77 *Life Watch*
Willis Barnstone

No. 78 *The Owner of the House: New Collected Poems 1940–2001*
Louis Simpson

No. 79 *Is*
Wayne Dodd

No. 80 *Late*
Cecilia Woloch

No. 81 *Precipitates*
Debra Kang Dean

No. 82 *The Orchard*
Brigit Pegeen Kelly

No. 83 *Bright Hunger*
Mark Irwin

No. 84 *Desire Lines: New and Selected Poems*
Lola Haskins

No. 85 *Curious Conduct*
Jeanne Marie Beaumont

No. 86 *Mercy*
Lucille Clifton

No. 87 *Model Homes*
Wayne Koestenbaum

No. 88 *Farewell to the Starlight in Whiskey*
Barton Sutter

No. 89 *Angels for the Burning*
David Mura

No. 90 *The Rooster's Wife*
Russell Edson

No. 91 *American Children*
Jim Simmerman

No. 92 *Postcards from the Interior*
Wyn Cooper

No. 93 *You & Yours*
Naomi Shihab Nye

No. 94 *Consideration of the Guitar: New and Selected Poems 1986–2005*
Ray Gonzalez

No. 95 *Off-Season in the Promised Land*
Peter Makuck

COLOPHON

Darling Vulgarity, poems by Michael Waters, is set in Centaur, a digitalized version of the font designed for Monotype by Bruce Rogers in 1928. The italic, based on drawings by Frederic Warde, is an interpretation of the work of the sixteenth-century printer and calligrapher Ludovico degli Arrighi, after whom it is named.

The publication of this book is made possible, in part, by the special support of the following individuals:

Kurt Brown & Laure-Anne Bosselaar
Alan & Nancy Cameros
Craig Challender
Gwen & Gary Conners
Wyn Cooper & Shawna Parker
Dale T. Davis & Michael Starenko
Richard Foerster
Suressa & Richard Forbes
Bev & Pete French
Dane & Judy Gordon
Howard Haims & Carole Cooper-Haims
Kip & Deb Hale
John Hoppenthaler
Peter & Robin Hursh   ✳   Robert & Willy Hursh
Steve Kronen & Ivonne Lamazares
Archie & Pat Kutz
Craig & Susan Larson
Rosemary & Lew Lloyd
Jimmy & Wendy Mnookin
Boo Poulin
Roland Ricker
Bob & Judy Sheridan
Ed Vates
Rob & Lee Ward
Dan & Nan Westervelt
Pat & Michael Wilder

No. 96   *Tho Hoopoe's Crown*
         Jacqueline Osherow

No. 97   *Not for Specialists:*
         New and Selected Poems
         W. D. Snodgrass

No. 98   *Splendor*
         Steve Kronen

No. 99   *Woman Crossing a Field*
         Deena Linett

No. 100 *The Burning of Troy*
         Richard Foerster

No. 101 *Darling Vulgarity*
         Michael Waters